Shadows Trail Them Home

Shadows Trail Them Home

Scott Owens & Priscilla Campbell

Copyright 2011 by Clemson University
ISBN 978-0-9835339-7-9

Published by Clemson University Press in Clemson, South Carolina

Editorial Assistants: Jacob Greene and Jared Jameson

To order copies, please visit the Clemson University Press website: www.clemson.edu/press

Contents

Acknowledgments • viii

ಞ

The Nature of Attraction

ಞ

A Lily for Sara • 2
Occupied • 3
Sara's Dilemma • 4
Sara Gone Wild • 5
The First Time • 6
Sara Never Needed the Sexual Revolution • 7
Normally Norman • 8
Belonging • 9
Child of the Wind • 10
Norman Warms to the Idea of Love • 11
Sara Discovers Norman • 12
The Nature of Attraction • 13
Norman's Enormous Thing • 14
Resizing Norman • 15
Norman's Stone • 16
Plunging Deeper • 18
Escaping the Storm • 19
Adoring Norman • 20
Quiet Like a Man • 21

ಞ

Norman Moves In

ಞ

Faithful Sara • 23
Norman Moves In • 24
For Sara • 25
Norman's Words • 26
Purple Breasted Women • 27
Routine • 28
Avoidance • 29

Album • 30
Loving Norman • 31
Sara Never Wanted Children • 32
Night Moon • 33
Mothering Sara • 34
Sentinel • 35
Confronting Paternity • 36
The Problem with Solutions • 37
Sara goes to a Psychic • 38
What Sara knew • 39
Taken • 40
Mother Love • 42
Likes and Dislikes • 43

☙

The Day He Left

☙

The Day He Left • 46
No Time in the Subconscious • 47
Unredeemed Souls • 48
Norman Appears • 49
Sara's Wabi Sabi • 50
Spotting Norman • 51
Take Out • 52
Norman Tries Again • 53
Drone Wings and Shoeboxes • 54
Six Now • 55
Back in the Day • 56
Unsettling Changes • 57
Descent • 58
Knots • 59
As If He Were Herpes, Global Warming, Greed • 60
The Boy • 61
Chance Encounter • 62

☙

Having Once Been Loved

☙

Quicksand • 65

Sara Dreams of Norman • 66

Norman and the Moon • 67

Tossed • 68

Norman Persists • 69

Trimming Norman • 70

Coda • 71

Loving Norman • 72

Phoenix Rising • 74

What He Wanted • 75

Having Once Been Loved • 76

Dining Alone • 77

Crucible • 78

Grown • 79

Without Words • 80

☙

Epilogue • 81

A Note on the Authors • 82

Acknowledgments

Grateful acknowledgment is due the following journals where some of these poems were previously published:

Blue Fifth Review for "Adoring Norman," "Back in the Day," "A Lily for Sara," "The Nature of Attraction," "Norman Persists," "Sara Discovers Norman," and "Sara Goes to a Psychic"

Charlotte Poetry Review for "Norman's Enormous Thing"

Future Cycle for "The Problem with Solutions"

Future Earth Magazine for "Dining Alone"

Gutter Eloquence for "Descent"

Main Street Rag for "Quiet Like a Man"

The Mom Egg for "Sara Never Wanted Children"

Nightsun for "Escaping the Storm"

Opium Poetry for "Letter to Pris" and "Loving Norman"

R-KV-R-Y for "Sara Discovers Norman" and "Sara's Dilemma"

Scythe for "As If He Were Herpes, Global Warming, Greed," "Chance Encounter," and "Trimming Norman"

The Shape of a Box for "Night Moon"

The Smoking Poet for "Resizing Norman"

Heavy Bear for "Drone Feathers and Shoe Boxes"

Empowerment4Women for an earlier version of "Belonging"

Outlaw Poetry Review for "Resizing Norman"

Waterways for "Album" and "Norman and the Moon."

"The Day He Left" was previously published in *The Best of Poetry Hickory* (Main Street Rag Publishing Company, 2011).

"Norman's Enormous Thing," "Norman Warms to the Idea of Love," and "Likes & Dislikes" were previously published as part of *The Fractured World* (Main Street Rag Publishing Company, 2008).

Many of these poems were previously published as a chapbook entitled *The Nature of Attraction* (Main Street Rag Publishing Company, 2010).

The Nature of Attraction

A Lily for Sara

Sara undresses by late moonlight,
paints a fluorescent-blue peace lily
on her belly, day-glo blue on her nails,
dances at her apartment window.

Cars slow to a crawl.
Passersby gawk.
One grey-bearded man yells
he's having a flashback,
tries to climb the smooth brick façade.

Sara's too young to have been a hippie,
but she's convinced her heart
is stitched from tie dyes
and faded blue bell bottoms.
She can't put flowers in gun barrels
so makes this statement instead.

Moody Blues, ELO, Fleetwood Mac—
they all make her lily sway harder.
The crowds thicken.
She makes the late night news,
flashes of nipple discretely edited out.

Novelty over, the street becomes quiet.
Sara finally sleeps, blue blending
into the early morning light.

Occupied

Oblivious to the blond
who has filled his glass
seven times, lingering
a moment longer on each trip,
dipping each time a bit lower
so that the rim of her shirt
reveals a bit more,
Norman can think only
of the girl he saw before
with colored breasts
just visible beneath her sheer
cotton shirt, blue paint
riding like water from one
breast to the other —
and not just any water but
ocean water as it moves
in low, hypnotic swells
behind barrier islands,
certainly still wild,
certainly still powerful,
but somehow under control,
somehow safe, somehow
somewhere that might be home.

Sara's Dilemma

Men follow Sara
down the street,
across town,
into her favorite
ice cream shoppe.
They would lick
her cone if she
let them.
Sara doesn't think
she's pretty, wonders
if she gives off a scent,
like cats do in heat.
Preachers especially
like her, seem to set
their god antenna,
spot her coming.
She asked one about
her existential struggles
and the true meaning of life.
He kissed her hard, hand
grazing one breast.
She finally fucked another
in back of his parish,
jockeys tossed to the ground.
Didn't know how to say no,
didn't want his white collar
looming. Did it, anyway.
Hoped in a perverse
sort of way if there really
was a hell this would ensure
him his ride there.
Men of god, she decided,
hadn't been around when
Christ made the scales fall.
She feels invisible,
wants men to want
more than sex. They never do,
so she reels them in,
lips puckered like guppies,
feels numb when it's over,
insides throbbing, blouse
wrongside out

Sara Gone Wild

The heart left alone gnaws at its own walls, wild animal in a trap of loneliness and fear.

Sara bedded them all
without shame or regret,
students and teachers alike,
clergy, cold accountants,
fiery musicians, each
with their own sort of power,
sometimes two or more
in the same night,
only washing in between,
the headache, the busy day
the only excuse she needed,
since they, a bit ashamed,
or fearful of discovery,
were always eager enough
to dismiss afterward,
the way a man after eating
moves quickly from table
to comfortable chair,
his business of dining done.

It was all too easy,
she thought, needing little
more than a quick smile,
willing eyes, short hair
framing the little girl face.
The legs she wore like lures
beneath her waist were nice
as well, but not really
necessary. A simple, "Come on,"
seemed always enough.

She was almost always
open to the possibility
of love, more often disappointed,
endurance not a strong point,
size unimportant,
sensitivity non-existent.
Sometimes, she said,
it had to do with joy,
sometimes pain or anger,
sometimes revenge, mostly
just with filling
what always seemed empty.

The First Time

The first time was in the bar
where he often went to be alone.
She might have been there before
but he never would have noticed,
keeping his head down, eyes
transfixed on perfect polish of surfaces,
stack of glasses rising before him.
And then a face appeared in the glass
stretched out like old Westerns
but smooth, perfect, unadorned,
eyes wide, mouth moving,
lips seeming to say *Here.*
Here. Is anyone sitting here?
And the glasses no longer mattered,
only got in the way of what
he knew he wanted to touch, to hear,
to look into like the first thing
that needn't be counted.

Sara Never Needed the Sexual Revolution

Sara never needed the sexual revolution
to tell her how things ought to be.
She had always dreamed of a place
where all the men smelled of Irish Spring,
had hands as big as ball gloves,
never said anything but *Yes*.
Sara invented her own revolution.
She knew what power her body held,
devised new ways to flirt,
turn a man's head, other things, too.
She could have them hot in a second,
loved watching them squirm
before she flipped one hand
through her hair, walked off
leaving them panting, happy
to think they had gotten so close.
It was the ones who stayed cool,
the refrigerators, motors purring
beneath metallic doors who appealed
to her the most. They were the ones
she dropped her own invisible guard for,
became what she always swore
she'd never be, not since that first time
someone made her do
what she hadn't wanted to.

Normally Norman

knows when to keep his mouth shut.
Normally Norman hides his head
anytime voices get raised.
Normally Norman wouldn't dream
of stepping in between a man
and the woman he brought with him,
but something about the night,
something about the red lingering
in her familiar cheek even when
the neon beer sign changed to blue,
something about the way her long legs
splayed out to keep her balance
and look the man straight in the face
as her eyes said, *I'll die
before I let you hit me again,*
something about the way the past
refused to stay in the past
made real for the moment
what could be, should be,
made real for the man
the sudden size of Norman's right hand.

Belonging

Sometimes Sara feels like an orphan,
imagines herself raised by Nuns.
Her grandmother never did like
Sara's red floppy hats, long hair,
calf-length skirts stitched with roses.
She wanted Sara's hair permed,
nails colored a proper pale pink.
Her grandfather used to say
Sara needed to find God, that she
surely would go straight to hell one day.
Sara figures God knows exactly
where he is and doesn't
need Sara to find him.
Sometimes, though, she wishes
she still belonged somewhere, wishes
she could see her mother again,
could remember her clearly.
She thinks she remembers her father
in the upstairs bath, shaving,
lightning bugs morse-coding
each other through darkening pines out back.

CHILD OF THE WIND

Sara was born from the wind,
sired by thunder;
her sibs, pouring rain.
She could hold colors in her hands,
mix them to form rainbows.

Sara still half-believes things
her beautiful long haired mother
told her before a drunk in a Honda
sent both parents spinning
into their new home in the sky.

Her grandparents tried to cage her,
tame her, clip her wings.
She escaped at sixteen, wonders
if grandpa still searches.

Sometimes when shadows
reach out too far, she climbs to the roof,
spreads her arms, birdlike,
sings to the sky over the howl
of cats creeping the alley.

NORMAN WARMS TO THE IDEA OF LOVE

Maybe it would be okay, he thought.
Maybe this warmth would last.
Maybe I could stand her hands around me.
It would have to be better than this.

He stopped sitting up at night.
He stopped counting the buttons
on women's clothing, started feeling
the weight their faces held on his eyes.

Maybe the way I feel when she speaks
wouldn't go away. Maybe her words
slipping against my words would make something new.
Maybe this nervousness is love.

He started sleeping on top of the sheets,
stopped burying memory,
thought about noticing flowers more.

Maybe I should give in to my body's bending
toward her. Maybe a kiss wouldn't be
so bad. Maybe she wouldn't laugh.

He'd leave his curtains open, his window.
He'd wear his shirt with the top button
undone. His heart beating stopped being
the loudest thing in his mind at night.

Maybe I'll see her when I get the chance.
Maybe I'll let her touch me without
pulling away. Maybe I'll touch her.

He started tasting the air again.
He stopped swallowing his dreams.
He started remembering himself.

Maybe I'll lie here and wait.
Maybe I won't have to say a word.
Maybe I can get away
without doing anything at all.

Sara Discovers Norman

Sara is flash lightning,
a loose wire,
her current not quite
touching ground.
She got a tattoo once,
pierced her belly button,
sewed roses all over her
size six baggy jeans.
She wishes she'd known
Janis Joplin, Martin Luther King,
and The Chicago Seven; she admires
people who walk outside circling wagons.
She's attracted to Norman.
In his Lands' End pressed slacks
and tailored shirts, he almost
blends in, but his shoes
are as scuffed as hers.

The Nature of Attraction

It wasn't just the way
Sara deviled her eggs,
heart-shaped pimientos
sacrificed on top.
It wasn't just her willow legs
that clearly went all the way up.
Norman moaned over both
of these in private fantasies
after just one date.

It was more than the way
her barely there breasts
rose like inverted teacups
beneath her thin cotton shirt,
more than caramelized onions
and fried bacon in her potato salad,
more even than how she groped
his leg while he drove
slowly, milking time
between destinations.

He liked her laugh,
her smile, the way
she sympathized with childhood
pains, the way she saw
to the serious heart of everything
but never let it get her down.
He liked the way she opened
herself to anything that came,
sound of birds, splash of water,
lying back in sand.

He loved most the way
she rubbed the back of his neck
when he bent over the sudden poem.
He thought all this
must mean love or something deeper,
though as for that,
he thought sex and cooking
might have been enough too.

Norman's Enormous Thing

He thought if he could give it to her
just once he'd be rid of it forever,
but no matter how he tried it kept
coming back, bigger, and always
at the worst possible moment.

At work, at parties, on crowded
streets and buses, almost anywhere
he came in contact with people
it would pop out, refusing to stay
hidden, rubbing against those
around him, pushing them aside.

At home it lay on top of everything,
always tense and too big for his body.
It sat erect at the table,
hung over the chairs, covered
the television, blocked the door,
ready to rise up between them.

Night after night he came to her,
his hands full of himself, hanging
from his body like a second head,
bloated and mean. Night after night
she gently punctured his bag of self-
importance, releasing just enough air
to breathe, to let him breathe again.

Resizing Norman

Sara's afraid Norman's too big,
afraid he'll split her in two
if he comes inside.
He presses against her hard
when they kiss, asks her
to hold it—she says no.
She knows what that leads to.

She once went with a man
almost as big as Norman, was cleft
into two Saras when he entered.
Reckless Sara, the one on the left,
one-footed it off to a biker's bar,
did a one-breasted striptease,
made out with wild bearded Bill Sloan,
before prim Sara tracked her down
and jigsawed them together again.

Sara wonders if Norman
could be resized, an odd sort
of cosmetic surgery, granted,
like paring an apple all the way 'round,
and shrinking that fearsome head.
She knows some women like men big,
but Sara feels root canal size
already. She's desperate.

She adores Norman, loves his blue eyes,
the way his hands, his mouth
make her giddy. She's tempted
to be two Saras again, buys
strong rope, handcuffs, duct tape,
just in case, then burrows,
mouselike, into her far larger hole
of wanton indecision.

Norman's Stone

Twenty-eight to his thirteen, half-drunk,
she lured him to her bed, pleased
herself with his finger, letting him
roll around on her ample chest,
deal with his prodigious problem himself.
For weeks after, he was terrified
she would tell her husband.
Or worse his father. He avoided her,
after that, avoided thinking
about what happened that day, almost
convinced himself it never did.

As he grew older it wasn't that Norman
didn't get horny. A well shaped breast,
a pretty leg, an inquisitive glance
all set him throbbing, but he couldn't
bring himself to do anything about it,
certain he had done something wrong,
would do it again, that everyone knew
the size of the problems he'd cause.

He wanted to release the tension,
dreamed of women who wanted
nothing more than the thrusting,
but always they turned to say *Stop*
with the same pained, irresistible face.

His heart became a stone.
He tried to feel, but couldn't
until in this desert of numbness,
he found Sara. Now he wants
to try again, to please her,
make her laugh, murmur *yes*.

He knows he's naïve, reads
sex manuals on the Internet for hours,
googles Masters and Johnson,
learns how, with the flick of tongue
or finger, to turn women on,
make them want more.

The Nature of Attraction

Nothing prepared him for that first time
with Sara, though. Her warm body,
trusting eyes, upturned breasts
all thrilled him, took him beyond
the place of memory or fear.

He studies Sara, listens for her gasps
when he moves one way, silence
when he goes the other. He tries
out the things he learns.
She teaches him, too, by her moans.
One night they go at it until dawn,
stopping only for water.

His fears stop haunting so much.
The numbness begins to ease.
Like some of her light reaches
into his darkness setting him free
for a while. Just looking
at her face does that, too.

Plunging Deeper

Sara thought Norman would be just
another passenger on that busload
of men traveling through her life.
He was awkward at first,
like a teenager in bed,
trying to figure what went where,
how best to kiss her.
She didn't know if he would last,
if she could overcome the fear
of his size. If she hadn't sensed
some connection, some unspoken bond,
she would've moved on.
It's been a week now
with Norman over almost every night,
yet suddenly it seems as though
he reads her mind, a driver who knows
which road to take without asking.
Stars burst in her head
when he's inside her.
She likes it when he uses
his tongue, too, long legs
looped over his shoulders,
while he explores her treasures,
arms flung over her head,
when she screams.
Too many men in her life
get wide-eyed when she lets herself go
so completely. They hurry off,
shirt tails flying, like she's
some misfit, not the coy
little girl they thought
she was when they met her.
Sara likes to please Norman, too,
watch his normal reserve ease
into a face that could dig its way
into her deeper than that other part
if she let it.

Escaping the Storm

During the storm they made love
by candlelight, bodies transformed
to golden, arched nearly to breaking,
limbs entwined, fingers fondling
curves and creases, coming wet
with each other, speaking in tongues,
bed shaking with pleasure, sheets
huddled in the corner, dragging on the floor.

When it ended, he couldn't wait
to clean up, take saw in hand,
separate limb from limb,
tie up loose ends of trees,
drag the random exhalations
of wind to a single pile for burning.

She was content
to lie in bed, surrounded
by wreckage, listening
to aftermath, mouth humming,
eyes closed, legs open,
still wet and moving.

Adoring Norman

Sara said she had poem envy
as she opened the fly-
leaf at the front of Norman's
latest book of poems.

Each image she felt
was harder than anything
she could manage
on her own. Every line

as well-hung as any
she'd ever seen.
His sackful of words
carefully metered

and plump with possibility.
She loved the way he
penetrated deeply
into any matter

that attracted him, varied
his pointed thrusts
for climactic effect,
remained always headstrong,

perfectly erect. She loved
the music of moan
and sway he pulled
from inside her, the way

he left her overflowing
with powerful feelings, spent
inside but never tired
of stroking his iambic ego.

Quiet Like a Man

Entering the room of this dream
he sees himself entering the room
of this dream. On any other night
he might have brought flowers,
but now the smell is that of burning,
the sharp arc of welding the door
closed. A man with yellow teeth
is surprised to see him here.
He doesn't understand he is
inside the room he is sealing.

He smells the things he dreams,
chews the tips of his fingers,
tastes the flesh beneath the nails.

A man's teeth will always be
as large as his fear. His eyes
show limbs scratching
against the window, hands reaching
out from the bed, the tight
shrinking of walls around him.

A boy's face rises from the cupboard,
a half-eaten apple, the skin of his arm
like an orange, ripe and ready
to peel, like the blown face
of water, broken, wrinkled, unable
to stop its own caving in.

He wants to be quiet like a man,
take his tears off into silence,
into shelter of trees. Rain falls
on his face and he wakes fresh
and covered with water. He doesn't
understand that everything he fears
is inside the room he is sealing.

Norman Moves In

Faithful Sara

Sara decides to try the path
of righteousness, go straight,
say no to men dogging her footsteps.
She thinks she can do it with Norman.
His big thing doesn't scare her
anymore—she's still intact.
She likes it when he stays
for breakfast, makes eggs
without breaking the yolk,
or when he pleases her first
with his mouth, not
just shoving it in.
She likes being on top,
wriggling her dance of desire
until shudders flare her again.
She rarely came with the others,
feels safe with Norman.
She doesn't know why.
Maybe it's the poems he writes her,
his perfectly trimmed nails,
or the careful way he touches her face.
Almost as if he fears a slap, not
a caress, might slip through
his fingertips, cracking their world,
fragile as this morning's eggshells.

Norman Moves In

Sara watches Norman unpack.
He brings in his toothbrush,
dental floss, razor and shaving cream,
four pairs of slacks, seven shirts,
underwear and socks.
He lines up his toiletries
in Sara's untidy bathroom,
labels facing front,
handles turned to one side,
scrubs down the tub when finished.
He adds she needn't worry about
the toilet. He always wipes
the rim after, lowers the seat.
His pants and shirts go to Sara's
hall closet, shirts hung facing
the same way, buttoned, coordinated
with the pants to be worn with them,
carefully creased across brown plastic
hangers he brought with him.
He sets jockey shorts, fly up,
precisely folded on a shelf.
Norman glances at Sara's closet,
clothes hung haphazardly, regardless
of type or color and the way she stuffs
her underwear and gowns down into drawers.
She can see this unsettles him.
She tries to refold, but it's hopeless.
Norman sits quietly most evenings
works on his poems, reads Chaucer.
She wants to get closer, know what he feels.
The mask he wears is too thick.
She strips off her blouse, steps
out of jeans, stands in front of him,
nipples peaked, panties damp.
He rises, eager to please, hands reaching
to touch, glad to know what's expected,
but when they climax and he thinks
she's not looking, Sara sees fear
beneath the lust on his face.

For Sara

he
made coffee every morning
breakfast
fed the cat
emptied the trash
opened windows she couldn't reach
folded clothes
mowed
planted a garden
weeded
picked parsley, rosemary, basil
vacuumed
put away dishes
organized cabinets
showed her house wren, cosmos, autumn joy
imagined being different
grew patient
listened
lingered
let go
even if only a little

Norman's Words

Norman's good at words.
On paper. They seem to fall
from the sky to his pen.
Norman isn't good at saying
how he feels, describing
how he sees things out loud.
He wants to tell Sara
she's beautiful, that he likes
the way she hums in the bath,
how cute her frown is when she concentrates.
Instead, he cooks their breakfast,
changes the sheets, puts away dishes.

Norman inherited his money
from an aunt who was a writer, too,
the only friendly face he remembers
from childhood. His mother's back
was always turned, running,
like a woman closing her eyes
in the bad parts of a movie.
Like Herod, no blood on her hands.

The money lets him write, lets him avoid
people, too. His aunt's biggest gift.
Norman writes Sara a love poem.
Maybe he'll show her, maybe not.
She might laugh. Maybe it'll scare her.
It scares him. Love is a beast
that can grow horns for the kill.
He tucks the poem away for now.
Safer to stick with breakfast.

Purple Breasted Women

Sara paints women with breasts
ten handfuls larger than hers,
paints those breasts green.
She dreams about a clan
of purple-breasted women
who never let a man stick
his heel in their face, force
them into submission, make them cry.

Sometimes she paints her own breasts
purple with eye shadow, imagines
women all over town doing the same,
locking arms, marching down streets,
tossing thorned roses at those
who dare jeer.

Her women go for a hundred a canvas,
more if the buyers meet Sarah.
Dressed in her long hippie skirt,
flowers in her hair, who can resist?
She's the real thing.
Doesn't have to cut off her ear
to prove it.

Drying canvases fill the room.
They unsettle Norman.
She pretends not to notice.
She wants to make Norman happy
but her purple breasted women stay.

Her next project is Norman.
She readies the canvas, paints
his enormous thing green,
sets an eagle on his shoulder,
wings spread wide, ready to fight
for Sara if need be.

An elderly woman from Brooklyn buys it.
For her bedroom ceiling, she tells Sara.

Routine

She paints.
He writes.
They cook together,
shop together,
shower together.
At night,
almost every night,
sometimes in the morning,
sometimes after lunch,
sometimes in the car,
they make love.

It all feels
ideal,
most of the time,
but sometimes she can't help
but notice
how he never looks
in the mirror,
and sometimes he can't help
but notice
how she always does away
with quiet.

Avoidance

Seven blackbirds on the lawn,
three cars parked on his street,
yes, Norman counted things,
15 strokes of the toothbrush
on each side, top, bottom,
front and back, 30 swipes
of deodorant beneath each arm,
a trick he learned years ago
alone in his room, 96
ceiling tiles, 37 cracks
in the sidewalk between home and school,
even beats and lines pleased him,
sometimes merely for distraction,
sometimes engaging a mind
he didn't trust to be unengaged,
sometimes his way of keeping chaos
at bay, socks sorted by color,
shirts by season, pants by purpose,
everything in its place and properly accounted for,
perceptible trends, patterns
analyzed for the sake of prediction,
preparation, justification,
knowing what might be coming
and how to avoid it.

Album

Norman is always looking away.
In every photo ever taken
he seems distracted by what just
happened behind him, off to one
side or the other or somewhere beyond
the photographer's shoulder or hand
saying *Look here. Smile. Cheese.*
And all you get are partial profiles
and inexplicably puzzled looks
almost as if he wanted to look
away, avoid the straight-on shot,
knowing the picture would never be right,
knowing none of it could ever be perfect.

Loving Norman

Sara hears Norman slip
out of bed before dawn,
sheets clammy behind him
She knows not to follow,
ask questions, or flutter
her fingers over his back.
She knows he won't hit her
like his father hit him
or do the unspeakable,
but he fears in dark
hours he might.
He's afraid his father will rise,
ghost from his dreams,
knock chair to floor, face mottled,
and slam with his fists
what palms held close
to chest earlier;
ripping apart all he holds dear,
burning his safehouse to ground.

Sara Never Wanted Children

imagined they'd slow her down,
had even been told she might not be able,
had planned her life around their absence.
Maybe that in itself had been enough
to justify in her own mind
her early reckless abandon.

She thought little of it when she was late,
didn't even notice until it was almost
the second month. When the home test
confirmed and the doctor made it certain,
she didn't feel the immediate joy
one might expect. Lost in a fog

of disbelief, she wandered past
her favorite haunts, coffee shops,
night clubs, all the places
she used to live, all the places
she'd been with men, waiting
for some meaning to be made clear.

Nothing came. No epiphany,
no purpose, no plan. Only a sense
of responsibility. Only that and fear,
fear that she wouldn't be enough,
fear of how this would change things,
fear of what it would do to Norman.

Night Moon

If I throw up I will die if I throw up I will die If I...

The words streak through Sara's head.
She presses her lips tight until the nausea passes.
Trying to overcome this inexplicable fear,
she bends, a broken tree, over porcelain,
legs quaking, hands forming a plea.

When she finally remembers him clearly,
she weeps: his old man's flesh
forced into her 8 year old mouth,
back pressed hard
against the narrow bed, springs creaking,
as he jerked his stench into her.

If I throw up I will die if I throw up I will...

She grieves for the child she forgot,
had to forget, but now
can no longer forget, nights
when her stomach churns
and the moon buries itself deep
into the innocent sky.

Mothering Sara

Sara was afraid she might drop a child,
feed it wrong stuff, not notice
sopping wet diapers.
She's terrified of childbirth,
white masks claustrophobing her
with push push, breathe breathe.
Childbound, she won't be able to run
in the rain, hold seances with fairies,
or disappear until dawn, floppy hat
drawn deep over her forehead.

Now Norman's child is inside, thumping.
She's seen the sonogram—he already has fingers.
She talks to her belly, explains
what a bad mother she'll be.
Wonders if he'll forgive her.

At the park, she lurks near the new mothers
to eavesdrop about diapers, formulas,
first steps, and magic first words like mama.
These women smell of lilac and powder;
their eyes glow with confidence.

Sentinel

Not even Sara knew how much
he watched until she saw the pictures.
She noticed it first in the one on the beach
that day in March. No one else there,
nothing going on but the stillness of the bay
behind him, what could he be looking at?
What might he see that she had missed?
And yet, the way he stood, head turned
to the side, seemed so familiar to her
she knew she had seen it before.
She went back through other pictures
and found it in every one, always
distracted eyes drawn to the side
or the horizon beyond the camera's shoulder.
She began to notice how often his eyes
didn't meet hers as they talked.
Only at home, in bed, could she keep
his focus on her. Anywhere else
it wandered towards windows and doorways,
anyplace the unexpected might come from,
always on alert, hypervigilant,
impossible to be in the moment,
as if danger lurked everywhere,
as if by watching he might see
what was coming and seeing
know how to avoid it.

Confronting Paternity

They talked about everything
or rather, Sara talked
mostly, and Norman listened.
They liked it better that way.
It worked. Except for poetry.
Then Norman did the talking.
Rhyme and meter, stanza
and image, conceit and poem-
length, onomatopoeia —
and children. They never talked
about children, not even when Sara
knew, not at first
at least, not until Norman
traced the curve of her belly
with his hand and his eyes lifted
to hers and penetrated
her silence, and then,
nothing. A numbness between
his eyes and empty mouth,
the static of drowned voices.

The Problem with Solutions

Even at 6 he knew he was smart,
smart enough, he thought, to figure out
how to avoid the backhand or belt buckle.
He told people, but nobody cared,
not then, not there, not in a place
that favored the rod, and not when the kid
had a dirty face and cut off pants.
He tried fighting back, but only
once as the hitting lasted longer,
the welts seemed deeper.
He even tried running away, twice.
Both times he woke up early,
snuck out before anyone else had stirred,
a paper bag stuffed with a change
of clothes, as much food as he could carry.
Both times he came back
before dark, a bit surprised
that no one had noticed him gone.
He stole cigarettes or money for revenge,
took pride in his quiet rebellion,
gave them to friends, big kids,
who never questioned the source.
But that never stopped anything.
He thought if he could master causes,
he could keep it from happening again.
He knew noise wasn't allowed,
breaking things bound to bring anger.
He learned to never talk back,
never touch anything without asking.
And things seemed to get better
for a while, but still, there was the random
smack or push when he walked by the couch,
the undeserved blame for lack of rest
or money, or time, the accusations
of smirks or eye-rolling, or improper tone
in the way he said, "Yessir," "Nosir,"
"I'm sorry." So he tried harder,
pulling his arms into himself,
keeping his mouth constantly shut,
playing alone in quiet corners,
trying to learn how to be invisible. But always,
when his old man finished with his mother,
his brother, he still came looking for him.

Sara goes to a Psychic

Sometimes Sara thinks
the dead speak to her.
She's sure her father
tells her Norman won't last.
Grandfather says she's no good.
An angel sits on the foot
of their bed some nights.
When Sara tries on her halo
everyone fades into the distance.
Sara loves Norman,
or thinks she does.
He still pleases her sexually,
often 2 or 3 times a night,
makes breakfast, painted
their bedroom, has started
doing her laundry. Her clothes
have never been neater.
Norman answers all of her questions
but holds some part of himself back.
A Black Hole, she teeters
on his precipice.
He rarely laughs, won't dance,
says it makes him look silly.
He's a good man...I'm lucky,
she tells herself and anybody
else who will listen.
She decides to go to a psychic,
holds out her palm,
covers the other's with silver.
She sees a cross.
She sees Norman hanging from it.
He's laughing.

WHAT SARA KNEW

The night Norman no longer lingered inside her,
Sara knew the past was back.
Persistent presence squatting on his brain
like guilt, fear, uncertainty,
it pushed him physically from her bed,
sent him to the window, the other room,
anywhere he could find a door,
a way out, space to breathe in.
She had seen it coming in eyes
that wouldn't be met, hands
that couldn't stand to be touched.
She knew it was nothing she had done,
and doubted there was anything she could do about it,
but when he held her in moments of passion,
and her own past dissolved into nothing,
she knew she had to try.

Taken

Sara finds Norman kneeling,
scrubbing the floor again,
shirt off, jeans riding low
on his hips, muscles of shoulder
and back rising and falling
as hands work in circles
his magic spell of cleaning.

Part of her wants to do nothing
but stand in silence and watch.
The stronger part moves closer
behind him, crouches down,
reaches one hand around him,
brushing across his chest,
extended finger circling
a pink ring of nipple,
just touching its tip.

She sees his hand stop,
feels his chest expand.
Her other hand reaches deeper
into the trough of spread legs,
feels his flesh rising
to hers, feels him turn
to see in her eyes what drives
this desire, the look that says,
I will take you as you are.

Her mouth already takes
the shape of his rising,
and as he lets himself
be taken, he climbs again
out of the past, wishing
it could stay this way,
knowing, even now, it can't.

*he never gave her
an answer — only silent
acquiescence*

Mother Love

Sara never expected the child
to mean so much. She'd seen small hands
binding her freedom, like tugging
at a longshoreman's knot, each struggle
docking her tighter to shore.
Instead, the child makes her lighter.
Sails raised, she floats through the days.

The boy eases that ache still inside,
the hunger never quite filled.
She loves Norman more for seeding this gift.
She never expected to set roots,
not when her wanderlust still rose
like the tide, not when she saw
women in long, colorful dresses,
feathers in their hair, twirl
down midnight-drenched streets.

Norman's hands clench and unclench
when the boy leaves his toys scattered,
dribbles his food, cries when tired.
It'll work out, Sara tells herself.
Doubtful, her dead father says.

Likes and Dislikes

Norman will tell you
he likes dogs,
but that's not entirely true.
He likes dogs the way
he likes children,
when they are quiet,
when they are soft
when he wants them
to be soft,
when they are playful
when he wants them
to be playful.

Norman will tell you
he likes women,
but that's not entirely true.
He only likes women the way
he likes children and dogs,
mostly quiet,
mostly soft or playful
when he wants them to be
soft or playful,
mostly only the way
he wants them to be,
mostly there
only when he wants them to be.

Norman will tell you
he likes food.
Norman will tell you
he likes money.
Norman will tell you
he likes work,
but only the way
he likes it to be,
only the way
he likes women
or children or dogs,
mostly there
only when he wants them to be.

Norman will tell you
he likes himself,
but that's not entirely true.
He likes himself
the way he likes children,
the way he likes dogs,
the way he likes women
and food and money and work,
mostly there
only when he wants him to be,
mostly in silence,
mostly in little pieces.

The Day He Left

The Day He Left

Norman tried.
No one could fault him with not trying.
He never hit her,
not once in three years,
not even after the boy came
at first, though he felt the father within him
rising every day, trying to disgorge itself
across the bed, the table,
the faces of those he loved.
And then the day came
when his head hurt,
and it was too hot outside,
and things had gone wrong all day,
and the boy was suddenly louder
than he wanted him to be,
and his hand shot out
just ahead of memory screaming, "No,"
and then shot out again
in a trail of resignation
when she came to his side.

Sara stayed.
He knew she would,
at least for now,
soul that fought hard against giving up.
But he knew it wouldn't last
having tasted once the thrill
of the familiar, like any addict
he knew he'd do it again.

Years later, old and alone,
he'd see it as his one success,
the woman he almost loved,
the day he left.

No Time in the Subconscious

Sara could have handled losing him
to another woman. She'd been there
before, knew she was vulnerable
to voluptuousness, quick wit,
the need for being needed.

Fighting that came easy to her
with Norman. She gave her all
anytime, anywhere because
she wanted to, because
with Norman, it felt good.

But she never figured out
how to fend off phantoms,
fear of what one might become,
shame, self-doubt, the almost
physical presence of loathing.

Unredeemed Souls

Sara is suddenly afraid of everything—
gray Chevrolets
the stray dog in the alley
her trashcan
the man selling flowers on Greene Street
her paintbrushes

She wonders if unredeemed souls
spin through the galaxy
like planets or moons, even space debris.
She wonders if grandfather is close now,
like Mars was last month,
still trying to grab her,
still wanting one last shot
at the child she used to be.

Norman Appears

Norman walks down Greene Street,
head ducked, collar turned up
against a drizzling rain.
The rose on his jacket sleeve
is faded and peeling.
Usually fastidious, he doesn't care.
Sara gave it to him.
Back when he thought love
would hold the pieces together.
Back when he thought he could shove
old dreads into a box and seal it.
He misses Sara, the scent
of cinnamon in the kitchen,
her big floppy hats,
the way she teased him.
He longs for her teacup sized breasts,
those long skinny legs and
what was between them.
He's horny all the time, but
he's not been with anyone since Sara.
Sometimes he watches her and the boy,
wonders if he should approach.

Would she brush him aside or would she
touch his cheek, reach up for a kiss?
He can't take that chance.

He turns down Madison, then on towards
the river where the moon will rise full
tonight, its reflection a beacon
for lovesick mermaids and tired, lonely men.
He'll sit in the dark and think about
what could've been. He'll remember,
and peace will settle briefly as he curls
into that space between being Norman
and the man he thought he could be with Sara.

Sara's Wabi Sabi

Sara is a soaked handkerchief,
high tide, a flood.
For months she mourns Norman.
She re-reads his poetry, sleeps
on his side of the bed.
Gradually the sunlight returns.
Excess water dries.
She gives extra clothes, dishes,
chairs to the Salvation Army,
rearranges what's left.
She digs out her 'wild Sara days' dresses,
sings along with Carly Simon.
Sometimes, when the boy sleeps,
she dances naked, drinks cocoa,
reads Alice Hoffman or Tom Robbins til dawn.
Friends say she's found her Wabi Sabi;
she's still Sara, but changed.
Norman thinks he gave her nothing,
but he brought back her heart.
She takes the boy's hand.
They run through the park together,
feathers in their hair, her skirt
dusting the ground

Spotting Norman

Sara rounds the corner with the boy,
feels goosebumps and knows
Norman is near. She never
quite sees him, just a hint
of his favorite soap a fleeting glimpse
of his shirt sleeve. His checks
for the boy arrive monthly.
No note.

He's become one of the spirits
who cluster around her regularly;
parents, grandparents, an uncle.
She feels crowded. Friends
beg her to talk to their dead,
reach her hand into the air and pluck
out some remnant. Like flowers,
they say. Sara always says no.
She feels like a caravan already.

The boy skips beside her, face
red from the afternoon chill.
'Step on a crack, break
mama's back', he chants.
Oblivious to Norman's lurking.
Oblivious to the spirits' murmurings.
Oblivious to Sara's quickening
pace. The setting sun
lingers, fastens purple rays
to the horizon. Like Norman,
it wants her magic to hold
endings at bay, but night
steps on its fingers.
Shadows trail them home.

Take Out

Norman appears at the door,
long after the boy's in bed.
Hands her Chinese.
Conflict rearranges his face.
Finally he nods yes,
he'll come in...
just for a minute.
It's like old times,
sitting with chopsticks
and noodles.
He's not ready to talk;
maybe the hot weather, a small comment
about his new book.
Unaware of the stops in-between
they're in bed,
clothes taking flight,
Noman thrusting,
Sara's legs vice-gripping
his back.
He fills something left empty
in her for so long
that she wants to beg him
to stay the night,
but doesn't.
The boy cries out as Norman enters
for the third time.
Sara rushes.
A nightmare.
Hair wet, sweaty,
eyes wide like Norman's,
he tells her about demons
who came to take him away.
Norman is gone when she returns,
bed made, kitchen cleared.
Were it not for the slight scent
of his aftershave, she would think
she'd been dreaming, too.

Norman Tries Again

Coat pulled tight around him,
head down, he drags his feet
along Madison and Greene,
past closed store fronts,
trash cans set out by the curb,
almost invisible in the darkness,
wishing even these
last lights were extinguished.

His date gave up hours ago,
went alone to the bar
whose name he can't remember.
Sweet girl, undemanding,
not ungorgeous,
she'll meet someone who thinks
only of her breasts
between his teeth, her smile
that says *yes* to now,
the ass she keeps tight by running
daily these streets
Norman walks alone.

He knows the sky yawns
above him, and to the east
the sea yawns as well.
He knows he is going nowhere,
has nowhere to go. He knows
he can walk to the edge of town
where the lights run out and disappear
into absolute darkness. He knows
he'll never walk far enough
to leave it all behind.

Drone Wings and Shoeboxes

Long-legged Sara,
sloe-eyed Sara,
breasts barely a mouthful
under her rose
stitched hippie dress,
waits for the door buzzer.
She keeps Norman's photos
in a shoebox now,
pulls them out only
when memories stalk hardest.
Tonight's drone,
like all the other drones
doesn't really want her.
Just the honey between her legs.
She doesn't care.
Her heart flew away with Norman.
Never came back.
She fills that hole
with drone wings,
abandoned honeycombs,
and the wail of clarinet
in the blues band
down the street.

Six Now

The boy watches Norman slip
through darkness.
He's almost forgotten his face.
But he's six now.
He knows how to climb on a chair,
pull down his mother's secret shoebox.
The photos bring back the scent
of Ivory soap, big hands lifting him high.

He's six now. He was smaller then.
Could his daddy still lift him?

His mother doesn't say much
about Norman, just things like
'Your daddy loves you'.
Stuff any kid would never believe—
he wouldn't have left.

Yes, he's six now, knows lots of things,
like what his mother does
with those goofy-eyed men.
He's seen them kiss her, hopes
he doesn't have to kiss girls
when he grows up.

He has his mother's eyes.
Everyone says so.
Old ladies tousel his hair,
ask dumb questions like,
'What's your favorite color?'.
He tells them puke yellow and vomit green.
They don't try THAT again.

His mother likes to shock, too.
His sitter told somebody that on the phone.
He asked Timothy in fourth grade
what shock meant. He likes the word.
Rolls it over his tongue like candy.
Wonders if Norman shocks people, too.

Sometimes he wishes Norman would slip
out of the dark and come inside.

BACK IN THE DAY

Before she became a mother,
Sara hung out on the square,
painting women with green breasts,
purple breasts, orange breasts,
men with indigo or violet eyes,
matching cock and balls.

She smoked weed with her subjects,
played coy with long-haired
boys, shirts open, stroked
their chests, rubbed their necks,
spun round in their arms
to the sound of Jimi and Janis.

Now she paints portraits
of little boys in ball caps,
sisters in lace, while mommies
talk on cell phones, plays
the safe, expected jazz,
James Taylor, John Mayer.

But sometimes after hours
or when business is slow
she pulls out her brightest oils,
turns on Jefferson Airplane,
lifts her shirt, paints sunlight
circling beneath her breasts.

Unsettling Changes

Sara thinks she's met someone.
He never stayed out all night dancing,
never painted roses on city walls,
doesn't write steamy poetry,
or wear jeans with holes in the knees,
patches stitched up and down.
He brings her broth when she's ill,
opens doors, touches her as he passes.
His hands are careful, eyes soft.
Ten years ago she would've found him boring.
Ten years ago she wasn't a mom.
He takes the boy to the zoo, movies,
baseball games, wants to marry Sara
adopt the boy. After all, Norman
hasn't been seen in years.
Sara doesn't know how that works.
She would have to face Norman.
Would her pulse race?
Would she want him again?
The boy's still Norman's son,
still that piece of Norman she wraps
her heart around like a pearl.
With the boy adopted, Norman may fade.
That part of her heart may collapse inward.

Descent

Norman sits at the dark bar,
head resting in one hand,
the other stacking shot glasses
into perfect pyramids, blissfully
unaware of comings and goings,
the song on the jukebox, particular
qualities of light, the bartender's boredom,
or the bottled redhead's lonely stare
that fixes him in place.
When he looks up he knows
immediately he hates her.
Rising, he doesn't hesitate
to lift one finger
and call her to follow along.

Knots

Sara takes out her never-worn white dress,
the one with daisies around the hem,
smooths it with her hand.
Memories travel up through her fingertips.
She planned to wear it the day
she felt for certain Norman would stay.
Sara believes in ritual, sometimes in magic.
She had meditated over the dress,
held it to her nude body in candlelight,
hand-stitched the daisies herself—Norman's favorites.
Now this new man, this man with kind eyes
and big feet wants to be part of her life.
She sits with the dress for hours,
asks for answers. It would be good for the boy.
He makes her moan in bed, reads
aloud to her when she's feeling blue.
The 'no' that finally comes isn't because
she still waits for Norman.
It's that Norman's knots were so tight
they helped loosen Sara's.
Now, when her stomach tightens,
thinking of prison walls and traps
set in the night, she needs to run
from all men, barefoot in the rain,
hair flying.

As if he were Herpes, Global Warming, Greed

Everyone had a solution for Norman,
psychotherapy, reality therapy, aromatherapy,
Prozac, xanax, lithium, liposuction.
His father would have said he needed
his ass kicked. One friend offered
to find his father and kick his ass.
More than one woman said
he just needed a good screw.
Sara thought love would work,
and he nearly found a safehouse in her arms.
Others said confession, penance, forgiveness.
He tried them all, but in the end
nothing could teach him to love himself,
could re-tie the knots left hanging inside.

The Boy

Sara sends the boy cards,
a baseball glove, a mitt,
signs them 'daddy'.
She doesn't want him to grow
without the love of a father.
When the boy asks, she weaves
different tales to explain
Norman's lingering absence.
The boy is older now.
Her stories cause shadows
to fall under his eyes.
Norman's eyes.
If Norman doesn't come
when he turns eight
she'll tell him, she vows,
then edges the age up to nine.
She wishes she'd told him
from the start, but words
stuck like clay in her throat.
She's only cared for two men
since Norman left. One reminded her
of wilder days, days when she
danced nude in her bedroom,
twirled scarves over her head,
painted roses over her guitar case.
The other man was quieter,
like Norman, but wasn't Norman.
She gave up men after that.
Maybe she'll start again later.
She misses a warm man in her bed.
She misses Norman.
Sometimes she cries, wonders how
he managed to burrow so deep.

Chance Encounter

Lately his chest seems to flutter
whenever he turns a corner.

He's sure he'll run into him
one day, stand face to face

like looking in a mirror.
He's watched him on occasion

over the years from a safe
distance, noted how much

taller he is than the others
his age, how his own red hair

peeks from under ball caps.
He figures Sara knew

he was there and let him
at least have this, knowing

he would never dare
endanger the boy again.

He's even allowed himself
a sense of pride seeing

passion, curiosity, drive,
tempered by Sara's gentle touch.

He wonders if he'll be able
to say *I'm sorry*,

if his chest will manage
to contain what lives there,

if it will matter
that he did it for him.

Having Once Been Loved

even years later
Sara's long legs still
stretch into his dreams

Quicksand

Whenever Norman sees Sara's window,
buildings tumble around him.
Cars crash
Stars crack, scraping scars
into the tender sky.
He always walks by late nights.
Never near a street light.
Sometimes he sees a shadow dancing
behind her pink shade.
Other times he sees two.
Whenever he thinks of trying again
(and he does...he still loves her),
his past becomes quicksand,
sucking him back to his father's voice,
'You're no good', the smack of closed fists.
For a while, with Sara, he felt safe.
Until the old horns blew louder.
Until he first raised his fist to stop them.

He lifts one foot to cross the street,
turn shadow to flesh again if she'll have him.
Lot's wife blocks his way.

Sara Dreams of Norman

He comes to her in the night,
stars in his hands, Venus
cresting his forehead.
He hands her the Milky Way,
a cover for her bed.
When he bends over to kiss her
his skin smells like baby powder.
His hands are feathers.
She wants him inside her again
fierce and rocking, but
when she blinks, he's already gone.
A star lies on her pillow.
Her bed lights up the room.

Norman and the Moon

stood still outside her window
for what must have been hours, stared
in silence hoping for a glimpse of anything
more substantial than shadow or memory.
Norman and the moon ignored the bay
of dogs, distant sirens, footsteps,
all the unknown sounds of night,
knowing nothing remained worth fear.
Norman and the moon it seemed
were one, or at least enough alike
to share some knowledge of solitude,
their only difference —
the moon shed light
Norman could only imagine.

Tossed

Sara feels tossed,
turned.
She's a salad.
She sees Norman again.
Head down, paper
tucked under arm,
they collide,
arm against chest,
feet struggling for balance
on this rainy downtown sidewalk.
His face mirrors their boy's.
Touching him, she feels a jolt.
He feels it, too;
he's trembling.
She's dated too many come & goers
these years since Norman.
She's tired of being perky Sara,
watching men's backs
when they've bedded and run.
She knows Norman still loves her
(she sees him passing some nights,
peering up at her window),
wishes her sword would kill
all of his demons.
She touches his face,
memory overcoming.
He takes her hand,
holds it, drops it,
begins to say something,
fumbles, stops,
then becomes another back
walking.

Norman Persists

In quiet hours he calculates things,
weighs days worthwhile against those
worthless, ponders possibilities,
a sleep without dreams, wonders
how the self would feel expanded.
He thinks things might be different somewhere
else and stands before the door,
hand grasping the handle, clutching
the curtain, peering through cracks in the wall
always on the verge of desperation,
needing a drink, courted by darkness
and suicide. What he has
is barely enough to keep him here,
but always it remains barely enough.

TRIMMING NORMAN

Once he started cutting
he wasn't sure where to stop.
Six inches shorter seemed
more manageable, and trimmed down
all the way around less frightening,
but he didn't want to go too far.
He remembered what Sara had said,
all the ways she found to love him
despite the enormity of it all.
He thought if she could take him the way
he was, then someone else might too.
He finally decided he'd had it long
enough, didn't need it anymore,
no longer had reason to dread
how much he might be like his father
without the beard and long hair.

Coda

Sara curls, a comma, around
Norman's old pillow.
Upstairs, young Molly Wilson
gets it on with some dark-eyed
myth-maker from the corner tavern.
The creak of their bed scrapes
chalk lines across Sara's ceiling.

Sara gave up singing her own mating
songs, longs now for a refrain,
even a three note riff
before the coda's arrival.
Norman brought her heart back
but again it beats an erratic rhythm.

She weeps into the pregnant night.
Her tears fall as golden rain onto
a passing tramp. He thinks briefly
of a girl he once loved,
then moves on down the highway,
his own song lost into the miles
disappearing behind him.

Loving Norman

is impossible.
He knows.
He's tried
for years,
hand stroking
his manly ego,
squeezing his bloated
throat.

Oh, he looks good
enough on the surface,
hair combed
across the thinning
spots on top,
teeth white
but somewhat bent,
cheap slacks pressed,
shirt immaculately clean
though a little damp.
Myrtle Beach Lothario
slightly out of season,
voice too loud,
sugar too high,
patience all but gone.

In his younger days
he tried hard
to earn the love
of at least one
warm body
beside him,
held his temper
in check,
spoke
only in whispers,
only sweet
words, tried
to be sensitive,
vulnerable, think
of others first.

Having Once Been Loved

He thought
if he could love
another, they might
love him in return,
but if his own father
couldn't do it,
if he, himself,
can't do it,
what hope
did anyone else have?

Phoenix Rising

Just when Sara believes
she'll never love anyone but the boy,
when she grows so weary the floor
collapses beneath her feet,
the purple breasted women appear
in a dream, commanding her
to dismantle her tomb of self-pity
and rise again like Lazarus.
Breasts purple beneath her blouse,
she runs in the park at dawn,
sees a man painting the sidewalk.
His eyes are violet, his feet big,
solid against the pavement.
Nearer now, she sees
he's painting a purple woman.

She squats down, adds purple breasts.
He looks into her eyes, adds roses
to nipples, then smiles. Her heart
moves suddenly like it once
did with Norman for this stranger,
this man she doesn't yet know,
but finds herself wanting to know.
Birds fly overhead, singing
their songs of possibility.

What He Wanted

The boy shoots up.
Sometimes it seems to Sara
that his head grazes the ceiling.
He hasn't mentioned Norman in years,
treats the violet-eyed man as his dad.
Like Sara, he paints, but blue
is his favorite color.

He won't let Sara into his room
for weeks, won't say why,
keeps his door shut.
It's not drugs-his eyes
aren't dilated or pinpoints—
and , god knows, he could ask
Sara anything he might want
to know about sex.

On Valentine's Day, he blindfolds Sara,
walks her to the open door of his room.
On the wall is a painting; man and boy.
The man's head is pale blue, his body golden.
His hand rests on the boy's shoulder.
Red hearts cover both chests.
To Sara, it looks as if they're all beating.
She waits for his comment.

It's Norman, he finally says.
It's how Norman wished we could be.

Having Once Been Loved

Older now, Sara still paints
in morning light nothing but women
with purple breasts, never fast
enough to keep them on the walls
of the downtown gallery that sells them.
She still talks to her son every day,
still goes to the park when she can.
She has known many men,
none better than this one
whose violet eyes grant her mornings
in sunlight, who built this room
of glass with his own hands,
who reads while she works, listens
when she speaks, joins her when she dances
to Dylan, who taught her son
to be kind, gentle, proficient.
And in every painting amid the purple
there stands the green shadow of a man.
She hopes his hands, having once been loved
have found the answers they need.

DINING ALONE

He sits in the familiar chair,
beneath the dim light,
feet raised, screen flashing faces
before him. He begins with a tossed
salad of regret, mix of shame,
indecision, lost opportunities.

He opens a bottle of loneliness,
pours just a little on top,
adds a dash of disappointment.
He stabs each bite with practiced
precision, each forkful
the perfect size for retching.

He moves on to soup,
a cold broth of unexpressed
emotion, the once-warm fat
now floating in brine.
He empties the bowl,
sopping it up with stale bread.

By now, he only picks
at the main course, memory
of the woman he left,
the son he expected too much of,
a side dish of insecurity,
choking on the final mouthful.

He washes it down with glass
after glass of self-loathing,
stacks the dirty plate
atop the previous days',
wipes his mouth on his sleeve,
his hands on the arm of the chair.

He eats it all in silence, knowing
what gathers at the back of the throat
can never be spoken, has to be spat
out like undigested meat.
For dessert, nothing,
an endless cup of solitude.

CRUCIBLE

Her crucible	His crucible
was the boy	
melting	casting
the solid past	the formless past
into something	into something
she could form	solid before him

Grown

Grown now, he's long limbed,
quiet, loves roses and feathers.
He counsels kids with suspicious eyes,
broken teeth, arms bound
in ominous casts, kids who've been
chewed up by lions, and spat out.

His mother told him about Norman
when he was sixteen. Now he's out
helping other Normans, trying to give
what Norman never got.

Violet-eyed man behind her, his mother
still runs in the park, skirt brushing
the grass and she's beautiful.
Men's eyes always follow, but she's oblivious,
her own demons subdued.

He watches for Norman everywhere.
Street corners, coffee shops, bookstores.
Sometimes, if he's lucky (or maybe
only imagining), a whisper rides
on the wind, says 'I love you, son'.

The stars seem brighter those nights
when they peek in at his mother's
purple breasted women, sentinels
on his living room wall.

Without Words

Their eyes meet over the heads
of the crowd gathered to hear
the renowned poet full of his youth
and vigor share language he thinks
has never been used before,
his asking if she's okay
as she totters against the wall,
legs seemingly uncertain beneath her,
hers full of sadness at how thin
he's become, how red
his face, how spare his hair.
They both know how much they care.
They both know how late what could
have been became possible again.

Epilogue

Letter to Pris

Sara and Norman aren't gone, of course.
They can never be gone completely.
When I walk alone under a waxing moon,
Sara is there, her hand in my back pocket.
When you try to rise, morning's drowse
stretched across your eyes, Norman
is there, pulling you back, wanting, needing.
When I hide my head beneath the covers,
making love until there's nothing left,
I know that Sara and Norman are there.
When you see the girls in cropped tops
and hip-huggers, long hair and strategically
placed tattoos, all breasts and thighs,
like modern-day fertility goddesses,
creating the world in their own image,
you know that Sara is there.
When I answer the alarm and press
my slacks and drive to work
in a hurry and stay late and worry
over every detail, I know that Norman
has come back without Sara this time.
When I hear from another room
that something in the voice of a man
in love, quiet murmur of assent,
hum of appreciation, ur-language of love,
I know that Norman has found
at least some temporary peace,
and even my own raging stops a moment,
stands still in the possibility of love.
Today, in the garden, Peruvian lilies
opened their petaled throats, and I swear
I heard Sara's voice singing
    We may never pass this way again.
What else could I do but listen and kneel down
and cry over things that pass and all
the things we know will last forever?

A Note on the Authors

The poems of Pris Campbell have been published in numerous journals. The most recent include *PoetsArtists*, *The Dead Mule*, *Outlaw Poetry Network*, *Rusty Truck* and *Wild Goose Review*. She has had six poetry collections published by the small press and has been included in a number of anthologies. Her most recent collections include *Sea Trails*, a riff from her trip down the east coast in a 22-foot sailboat, published by Lummox Press, and *Postscripts to the Dead*, published by MiPOesias Publishing. One of her poems is featured in *The Poet's Market 2013*. Nominated three times for a Pushcart Prize and numerous Best of the Net awards, she also was recently contacted by Pearson Publishing for permission to include one of her poems in their next textbook alongside Margaret Atwood. A former Clinical Psychologist, she has been sidelined by ME/CFS since 1990 and makes her home in the greater West Palm Beach, Florida. Her website is www.poeticinspire.com.

Scott Owens is the author of 10 collections of poetry. His prior work has received awards from the Academy of American Poets, the Pushcart Prize Anthology, the Next Generation/Indie Lit Awards, the North Carolina Writers Network, the North Carolina Poetry Society, and the Poetry Society of South Carolina. His more than 1,100 published poems have been in *Georgia Review*, *North American Review*, *Chattahoochee Review*, *Southern Poetry Review*, *The South Carolina Review*, *Poetry East* and elsewhere. He is the founder of *Poetry Hickory*, editor of *Wild Goose Poetry Review* and *234*, and vice president of the Poetry Council of North Carolina and the North Carolina Poetry Society. He has taught at the college, high school, middle school, and community levels for more than 25 years. Born and raised in Greenwood, South Carolina, he currently teaches at Catawba Valley Community College in Hickory, North Carolina.

www.ingramcontent.com/pod-product-compliance
Lightning Source LLC
Chambersburg PA
CBHW031125160426
43192CB00008B/1111